English National Ballet

Like so many dancers, I have been dancing since I was five years old and it has been my passion ever since. I found dance by accident. My mother was a working mother and one day she was late picking me up. It was a very wet day and one of the teachers at my school told me to wait inside the gym - they were doing a ballet class. I had never seen ballet before, and I fell completely and instantly in love with it.

Ballet was for me an oasis. A place of music and beauty, where effort, dedication and passion were rewarded. I have always strived to open this wonderful and transformative world to everyone, everywhere, and specially to children.

This is why so much of my work at English National Ballet has been focused on expanding the diversity of those who create and participate in our art form - from commissioning to teaching and to reaching out into the communities in London and across the UK where we tour, to introduce ballet and invite all to be part of it.

It is equally important to know our own history and to honour those before us who have done the good work and whose legacy must be carried forward. This is why I am so proud to be supporting the work of the Black British Ballet project.

Ballet is a global language, one that should never be reserved for the few. What and who we see on our stages must be representative of the world we live in; this includes the stories we want to tell and the people who tell them.

I want to thank the Black British Ballet project for including me and ENB in this wonderful book and I look forward to seeing how children to explore ballet through its beautiful pages.

Tamara Rojo
Artistic Director, English National

BLACK
BRITISH
BALLET

I'm Dr Sandie Bourne and I hope you'll enjoy the story of Onisere's journey through the history of black British ballet. Black dancers have been present in British ballet from at least the 1940s. Among the early dancers were Jamaicans Berto Pasuka and Richard Riley who founded Europe's first black dance company Les Ballets Nègres in 1946.

When black British dancers started to train in the major ballet institutions in the 1970s, they were told that they would not be hired because they were black. So dancers like Brenda Garratt-Glassman, Carol Straker, Julie Felix, Michael Moor, Rachel Afi Sekyi, Adam James, Adesola Akinleye, Mark Elie and others went to work abroad in companies like Dance Theatre of Harlem and Alvin Ailey American Dance Theater.

Scottish Ballet was the first British company to employ Vincent Hantam in the 70s but it was not until the mid-80s that dancers like Brenda Edwards, Noel Wallace, Denzil Bailey, Ben Love, Simon Archer and Darren Panton began to find success in other British ballet companies. This is why Cassa Pancho founded Ballet Black in 2001, to create more opportunities for black British dancers.

I am delighted to be working with Oxygen Arts, English National Ballet, The Royal Ballet and Birmingham Royal Ballet as well as a range of other partners on the Black British Ballet project, which aims to celebrate the careers of black dancers in British ballet.

We will create a film and website that showcases their achievements and experiences, and inspires a whole new generation of black British ballet dancers, just like Onisere!

Dr Sandie Bourne
Black British Ballet
www.blackbritishballet.com

'I beg your pardon, young man!' bellows a terrifying voice from the sky. 'What did you say?' 'Um...er...ahh...' stumbles Tayo. Onisere claps her hand over his mouth. 'Ballet is most definitely, most certainly, most categorically for us all, you repellent little infant!' says Simbira, kissing her teeth.

'Come' she commands and scoops them both up. Tayo tugs her fingers, trying to get free then collapses on her hand. 'Dizzy!'

'Er, excuse me, aunty?' Onisere ventures. 'I don't mean to be rude but, who are you?'

She then gets excited and starts to jump up and down. 'Are you my fairy godmother? Are you here to make all my dreams come true? Are you? Are you? Are you?' she squeals with glee.

'Stop that nonsense right now! Do I look like a genie to you?' barks Simbira. Tayo opens his mouth but then snaps it shut again before she spots him.

'I am Simbira, Queen of Ballet, darling of the Russian stage, desired and adored by princes around the world and, of late, an overworked guide to ungrateful brats who think they know better than their elders!'

40s

60s

80s

70s

00s

50s

90s

Onisere gulps. Tayo, unfazed,
plays keepy uppy with his football.
Simbira begins again.
'Now where was I? Ahh, yes, far from being
an art form only for...' she hesitates,
'...people of the paler persuasion. There
is a long and impressive history of black
and brown people in British Ballet that
stretches back to the 1940s.'

Simbira waves her hand and almost dislodges the children.
'This is Les Ballets Nègres, Europe's first black dance company which
was started in 1946 in London by Jamaican dancers Berto Pasuka and
Ritchie Riley. Riley trained with my dear friend Margot Fonteyn you
know.' she confides. Tayo shrugs and Onisere looks blankly back at her.
'Oh never mind!' she says crossly.

'Then came Christian Holder, who was just perfection!' she kisses her fingertips. Tayo copies her but Simbira spots him, flicks him off her hand and continues, without a care. 'He came from Trinidad to London and then to Martha Graham before becoming one of Joffrey Ballet's most iconic dancers in 70s' New York. Richard Majewski came along soon after and he went to Zurich, Paris and then on a world tour with Béjart Ballet.'

'Next we had dear Vincent Hantam from Cape Town. He was so elegant and one of the hardest working dancers in ballet. He got a scholarship to the Royal Ballet School in 1972 and then joined Scottish Ballet. Greta Mendez from Trinidad went there too but they never met.'
'Why is he shivering?' asks Tayo as he drags himself back into her hand.
'Because Glasgow is a very cold city especially if you're from South Africa, you nincompoop!'

'In the 70s and 80s, most British ballet companies wouldn't hire black dancers but they were determined to dance! So people like Brenda Garratt-Glassman, Carol Straker, Michael Moor and Henderson Williams went to Arthur Mitchell's Dance Theatre of Harlem in New York City.'

'Wow' says Onisere, looking around.
'Wowee' says Tayo, finally impressed.

'Yes, but it wasn't all glamorous. New York could be quite a scary place back then, especially for a young person far from home.'
'Ugh, what's that smell?' asks Onisere, screwing up her nose.
'Ah, yes. The delightful aroma from 17 days of uncollected rubbish. The binmen went on strike in the winter of '81.' explains Simbira.
'Ewh! What a pong!'

'This isn't the Olympics!' says Onisere.
'No, c'est Le Opéra de Paris!' gushes Simbira.
'What's she on about?' whispers Tayo.

'Nureyev, you, you, you philistine!' splutters Simbira. 'Nureyev plucked Patrick Williams out of Alvin Ailey's company in New York and brought him to Paris where he wowed audiences for over five years.'

'Madiba!' breathes Simbira reverently.
'Johannesburg, '92. Adam James joined Dance Theatre of Harlem on their tour of the newly freed South Africa. I think Mandela had a bit of a crush on me but he had a country to rebuild and I was wedded to ballet!'
Tayo pretends to throw up behind her back.

Onisere starts to look a bit worried.
'So do I HAVE to leave home to be a ballet dancer?'
'You must be mad! America's awesome! They have the best music, cool cars and they SUPER size everything!' says Tayo.
'Silence, urchin.' says Simbira.

'If you strive for a little patience, I was just getting to the part where black dancers began to work more often in the UK...'

B 4 LL3T

'Ooh, who's he?' interrupts Tayo. 'Is he a footballer? Is he a rapper?' Simbira wrinkles her nose.
'No. That would be Darren Panton meeting Princess Diana. He was the first black British male dancer to graduate from the Royal Ballet School in 1992. Stunning dancer, dubious dress sense.'

'Did he get to dance in England?' asks Onisere.
'Yes, he joined London City Ballet when he graduated. They also had other black British dancers like Ben Love and Simon Archer. Ben trained to be a footballer with Everton, I believe.'

'Really?' says Tayo, getting excited.
'Yes, but he found he much preferred ballet.' she says smugly.
Tayo sticks his tongue out at her as soon as she looks away.

'Then we have the wonderful Brenda Edwards who joined English National Ballet in 1986 as their first black female dancer, while Noel Wallace became their first black male dancer a year earlier. Both their families were originally from Jamaica.'

'Did they have dreadlocks, like me?' asks Tayo eagerly.
Simbira pauses for a long moment.
'No, they did not, child.' she says gently.

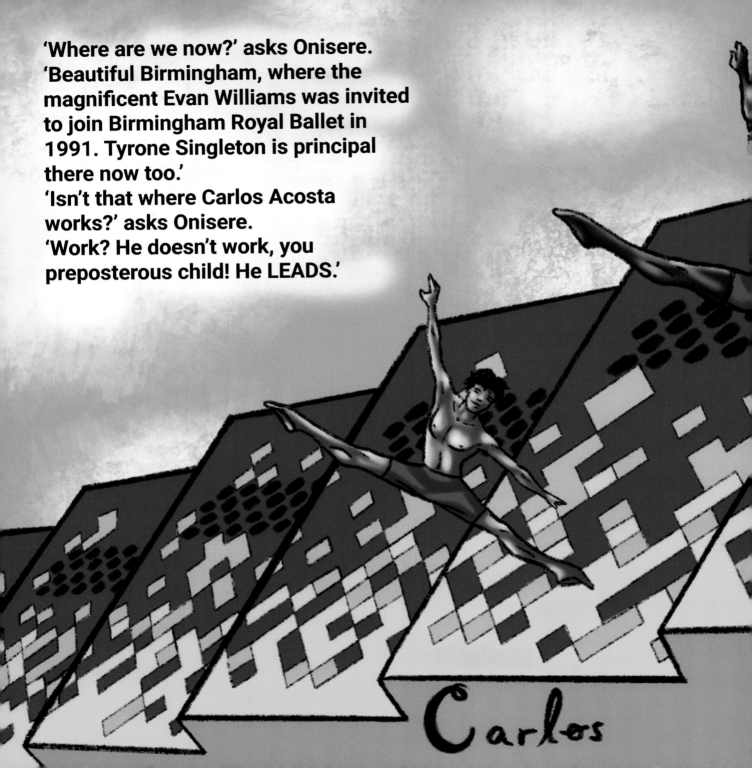

'Where are we now?' asks Onisere.
'Beautiful Birmingham, where the magnificent Evan Williams was invited to join Birmingham Royal Ballet in 1991. Tyrone Singleton is principal there now too.'
'Isn't that where Carlos Acosta works?' asks Onisere.
'Work? He doesn't work, you preposterous child! He LEADS.'

Carlos

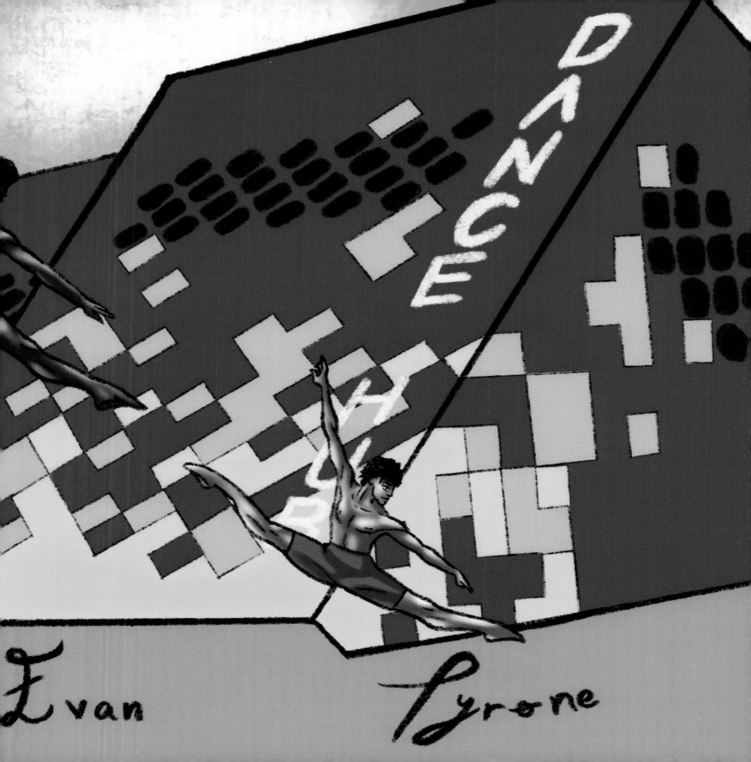

'Ooh, ooh, ooh, I know where we are now! This is the Royal Opera House!' says Onisere.
'Yes, we end our journey in Covent Garden, home of The Royal Ballet.'
'There are DEFINITELY no black dancers here.' says Tayo.

'Wrong again, smartypants!
Eric Underwood, Francesca Hayward
and Solomon Golding, among others, all
made their home at The Royal Ballet in
the last 20 years.'

Simbira drops the two children back in their bedroom.
'So what you're saying is that there have been loads of black ballet dancers...
AND that if I train really hard...
AND I believe in myself...
AND I never, ever give up...
THEN with a bit of help from my family and friends...
I CAN BECOME A BALLET DANCER!' says Onisere.
'Duh!' says Tayo, bored.
'Double duh.' says Simbira, flicking them off her hand and back onto the bed.